Colors of Fall

by Laura Purdie Salas

CAPSTONE PRESS
a capstone imprint

Fall is a season of change. Summer ends and school begins. Days get shorter, and the air turns cooler. Leaves drop from trees. Animals get ready for winter. Many fall changes include color changes too. Let's take a look at the colors of fall.

School is starting! Climb on your **yellow** bus and say hi to your driver. The same color covers school buses all over the United States and Canada. This color was chosen back in 1939. Its official name is "National School Bus Glossy Yellow."

5

Have you eaten a juicy **red** apple today? More than 2,500 kinds of apples grow in the United States. Red Delicious is one of the most popular kinds. Each fall, growers pick apples by hand. Fresh apples appear at the store, in your kitchen, and maybe in your lunch.

The **blue** autumn sky is cold and crisp. If you hear honking overhead, look up. Canada geese make a dark *V* against the sky. They are flying south for winter. When they're in a hurry, Canada geese can fly 1,500 miles (2,400 kilometers) in a single day.

Many flowers dry up and turn brown as days grow shorter and cooler. But not these **purple** mums! Chrysanthemums bloom from late summer into fall. They grow in other colors too, like deep red, gold, and bronze.

Fall means football. Hike! The quarterback has the **brown** football. Will he pass it, run with it, or hand it to another player? He wants to move the ball down the field and score a touchdown. Just don't drop it!

All summer, sunshine and green chlorophyll in leaves help trees make their own food. When the days grow shorter, trees stop making food. The chlorophyll fades away. Then the gorgeous **gold** and brilliant **orange** colors that were underneath can show through.

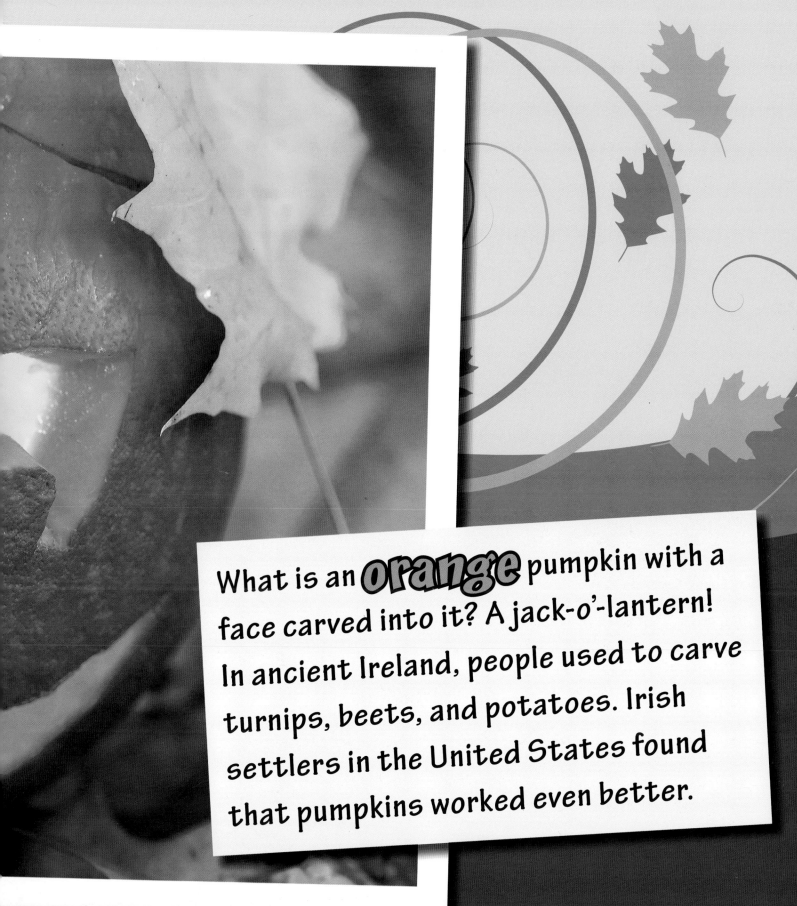

What is an **orange** pumpkin with a face carved into it? A jack-o'-lantern! In ancient Ireland, people used to carve turnips, beets, and potatoes. Irish settlers in the United States found that pumpkins worked even better.

Caw! Caw! Have you seen crows on the bare fall branches? Some inky **black** crows fly south for the winter. But they don't fly in neat *Vs*. They fill the skies in noisy groups of hundreds or even thousands of crows.

What's that **pink** thing? It's called a wattle. It makes male turkeys look good to females—really! Wild turkeys spend most of their time on the ground. If they need to escape predators, they can fly short distances. In the fall you'll probably see a turkey on your Thanksgiving plate.

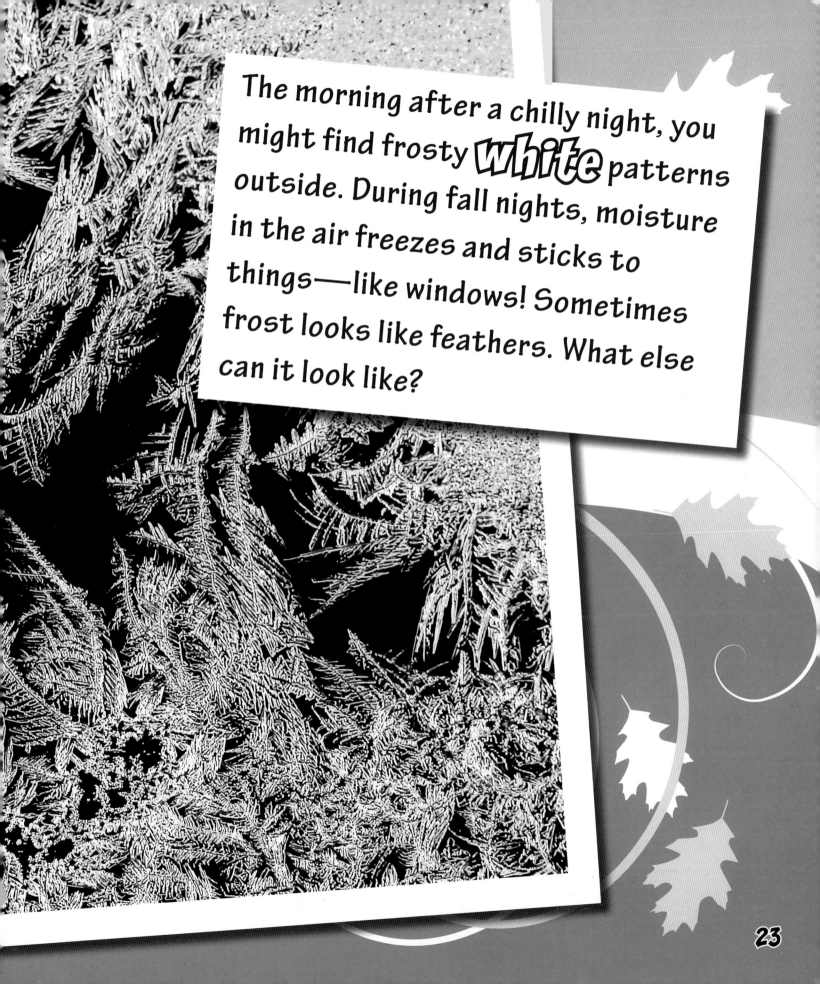

The morning after a chilly night, you might find frosty **white** patterns outside. During fall nights, moisture in the air freezes and sticks to things—like windows! Sometimes frost looks like feathers. What else can it look like?

Farmers harvest crops like corn and wheat in the fall. They use machines like this dark **green** combine to gather the **golden** corn plants. A combine can pick just the ears of corn and then remove the husks. It even takes the corn kernels off each ear!

Gray squirrels scamper around all fall. They hunt for acorns and berries to hide. In winter they will need the food. Squirrels don't remember their hiding spots. But they have a great sense of smell. They sniff out their stored treats, even once snow covers them.

The autumn equinox brings shorter days and longer nights. Nightfall arrives earlier and earlier. But as the sun sets, the city lights up. Like an artist's canvas, the world is flooded with color. How many colors do you see?

Glossary

chlorophyll—the green substance in plants that uses light to make food from carbon dioxide and water

chrysanthemum—a type of flower with various shapes and colors that has many usually small petals

equinox—one of the two days in the year when day and night last exactly the same length of time all over the world

quarterback—in football, the player who leads the offense by passing the ball or handing it off to a runner

settler—a person who goes to an empty or unknown area to live there

Read More

Emerson, Carl. *The Autumn Leaf.* Read-It! Readers. Minneapolis, Minn.: Picture Window Books, 2009.

Rustad, Martha E.H. *People in Fall.* All about Fall. Mankato, Minn.: Capstone Press, 2008.

Smith, Sian. *Fall.* Seasons. Chicago: Heinemann Library, 2009.

Internet Sites

FactHound offers a safe, fun way to find Internet sites related to this book. All of the sites on FactHound have been researched by our staff.

Here's all you do:

Visit www.facthound.com

Type in this code: 9781429652568

Super-cool stuff!

Check out projects, games and lots more at
www.capstonekids.com

Index

apples, 7
black, 18
blue, 8
brown, 13
buses, 4
Canada geese, 8
chrysanthemums, 10
corn, 25
crows, 18
equinox, 28
football, 13
frost, 23
gold, 10, 15, 25
gray, 27
green, 25
jack-o'-lanterns, 17
orange, 15, 17
pink, 21
purple, 10
red, 7, 10
school, 2, 4
squirrels, 27
Thanksgiving, 21
trees, 2, 15, 18
turkeys, 21
white, 23
yellow, 4

A+ Books are published by Capstone Press,
151 Good Counsel Drive, P.O. Box 669, Mankato, Minnesota 56002.
www.capstonepub.com

Books published by Capstone Press are manufactured with paper
containing at least 10 percent post-consumer waste.

Library of Congress Cataloging-in-Publication Data
Salas, Laura Purdie.
  Colors of fall / by Laura Purdie Salas.
    p. cm.—(A+ books. Colors all around)
  Summary: "Simple text and photographs illustrate the colors of fall"—Provided by publisher.
  Includes bibliographical references and index.
  ISBN 978-1-4296-5256-8 (library binding)
  ISBN 978-1-4296-6151-5 (paperback)
  1. Autumn—Juvenile literature. 2. Color—Juvenile literature. I. Title. II. Series.
  QB637.7.S25 2011
  508.2—dc22
                                                        2010028415

Credits
Jenny Marks, editor; Bobbie Nuytten, designer; Svetlana Zhurkin, media researcher; Eric Manske,
    production specialist

Photo Credits
Digital Stock, cover, 14–15
Getty Images/Blend Images/Jasper Cole, 2–3; Steve Smith, 8–9
iStockphoto/Andrew Howe, 18–19; Michael Krinke, 12–13
Shutterstock/Alexey Buhantsov (background), throughout; Artbox, 6–7; Bryan
    Eastham, 10–11; Cheryl Casey, 4–5; Clayton Thacker, 24–25; Elena
    Elisseeva, 1; F. Mann, 16–17; Gary718, 28–29; Geoff Hardy, 22–23; Patries,
    20–21; Sharon Day, 26–27

Note to Parents, Teachers, and Librarians
The Colors All Around series supports national arts education standards related to identifying colors in the environment. This book describes and illustrates colors seen in autumn. The images support early readers in understanding the text. The repetition of words and phrases helps early readers learn new words. This book also introduces early readers to subject-specific vocabulary words, which are defined in the Glossary section. Early readers may need assistance to read some words and to use the Table of Contents, Glossary, Read More, Internet Sites, and Index sections of the book.

Printed in the United States of America in North Mankato, Minnesota.
092010   005933CGS11